LEADERSHIP PRACTICES INVENTORY–INDIVIDUAL CONTRIBUTOR [LPI–IC]

Second Edition

Participant's Workbook

James M. Kouzes

Barry Z. Posner, Ph.D.

Jossey-Bass
Pfeiffer

San Francisco

Published by:

350 Sansome Street, 5th Floor
San Francisco, California 94104-1342
(415) 433-1740; Fax (415) 433-0499
(800) 274-4434; Fax (800) 569-0443

Visit our website at: http://www.pfeiffer.com

Outside the United States, Pfeiffer products may be purchased from the following Simon & Schuster International Offices:

Simon & Schuster (Asia) Pte Ltd
317 Alexandra Road
#04-01 IKEA Building
Singapore 159965
Asia
65 476 4688; Fax 65 378 0370

Prentice Hall/Pfeiffer
P.O. Box 1636
Randburg 2125
South Africa
27 11 781 0780; Fax 27 11 781 0781

Printing 10 9 8 7 6 5 4

Prentice Hall
Campus 400
Maylands Avenue
Hemel Hempstead
Hertfordshire HP2 7EZ
United Kingdom
44(0) 1442 881891; Fax 44(0) 1442 882288

Prentice Hall Professional
Locked Bag 531
Frenchs Forest PO NSW 2086
Australia
61 2 9454 2200; Fax 61 2 9453 0089

CONTENTS

Chapter 1 What You Will Gain from the LPI-IC 1

Chapter 2 The Five Practices of Exemplary Leadership 4

Chapter 3 What the LPI-IC Measures 6

Chapter 4 How to Analyze and Interpret LPI-IC Feedback 10

Chapter 5 Interpreting Your Own LPI-IC Feedback 24

Chapter 6 Summarizing Your Feedback 54

Chapter 7 Continuing Your Leadership Development 56

Chapter 8 Making Action Plans 78

Chapter 9 Discussing Your LPI-IC Feedback with Others 81

Appendix A Recommended Readings A-1

Appendix B Instructions for Hand Scoring B-1

CHAPTER 1

What You Will Gain from the LPI-IC

There's a popular myth that only a lucky few can decipher the mystery of leadership. But we've been researching leadership for more than fifteen years, and our research has demonstrated consistently and conclusively that leadership is not a mystery. We've gathered a huge amount of data—from more than 3,000 cases and 100,000 surveys—showing that leadership is an observable, learnable set of practices.

After assessing all of this information, the conclusion we've come to is this: *Leadership is everyone's business.* It's not just the business of managers and supervisors. Everyone must function as a leader at some time and in some arena—whether in an organization,[1] an agency, a task force, a committee, a community group, or even a family setting—and everyone can learn to lead effectively.

In keeping with our conclusion, we wanted to provide enhanced educational and training tools that would help *liberate the leader in everyone.* That's why we wrote a second edition of our foundational book, *The Leadership Challenge,* and why we've continued to develop and improve our instrument, the *Leadership Practices Inventory (LPI),* which assesses the leadership behaviors of managers.

That's also why we've improved the *Leadership Practices Inventory—Individual Contributor (LPI-IC).* This instrument is intended for people who are not in managerial positions but who lead all kinds of teams—teams that develop new products, cut costs, redesign processes, plan charity events, organize community-cleanup programs, and so on.

Now that you're about to complete the LPI-IC process, you'll be working toward liberating the leader in yourself. Regardless of your level or type of leadership experience, you'll find that completing the LPI-IC process will give you valuable insights about yourself as well as practical, useful information that will help you to realize your full leadership potential.

---

[1]*Throughout this workbook you'll see the term "organization." You can read this term as "company," "agency," "project team," "community group," or whatever your particular leadership arena happens to be.*

WHAT YOU CAN EXPECT

By completing the LPI-IC self-development process, you can expect to:

- Learn the five fundamental practices of exemplary leadership

- Receive valid and reliable feedback about your current use of these practices

- Find out how others perceive you

- Identify your leadership strengths and opportunities for improvement

- Find specific suggestions on how to improve in each of the five leadership practices

- Make action plans for continuing your leadership development

- Learn a process for discussing your feedback with others

WHAT'S IN THIS WORKBOOK

Here's what you'll find in this workbook:

- A brief explanation of the development of the LPI-IC

- Descriptions of the five practices of exemplary leadership

- An explanation of how to analyze and interpret LPI-IC feedback

- Questions that guide you through a detailed analysis of your own feedback

- More than 100 ways to improve your day-to-day use of the leadership practices

- Action-planning forms to complete so that you can direct your efforts to improve

- A suggested design for conducting a meeting with the people who gave you the gift of feedback, so that you can learn even more from them

- A list of recommended readings to further your leadership development

WHAT WE WISH FOR YOU

We wish you continuing success as you strive to meet your own leadership challenges. You'll discover, as we did, that leadership is essential not just in your career but in all of your relationships with others. When people succeed in improving their use of the five leadership practices, they enhance their contributions to their organizations and to their families and communities as well.

We trust that the LPI-IC will serve as a useful compass as you make your journey toward self-discovery and self-development. And we thank you for taking us along.

James M. Kouzes
San Jose, California
March 1997

Barry Z. Posner
Santa Clara, California
March 1997

CHAPTER 2

The Five Practices of Exemplary Leadership

When we decided to research leadership, we chose not to focus on famous military or political leaders, CEOs of corporations, or those who make headlines. What we wanted to know was how ordinary people accomplished *extraordinary* things in organizations. These were the people, we believed, who could demonstrate that leadership was accessible to everyone. So we concentrated on folks whose daily lives consisted of such activities as leading projects, managing departments, starting small businesses, and promoting community-based campaigns.

We began by developing a questionnaire that we called the "Personal-Best Leadership Experience." Hundreds of people completed the questionnaire, and we interviewed many more, using the questionnaire as a basis for our interviews. Each person was asked to select a project, program, or significant event that represented his or her "personal-best" leadership experience. Then the person answered specific questions about that experience. Here are some examples of the questions we used:

- What made you believe you could accomplish the results you wanted?

- What did you do to get other people involved in the project?

- What strategies did you use to encourage others to "stretch" in their efforts to meet project goals?

- What key lessons about leadership did you learn from the experience?

Despite the differences in people's individual stories, the personal-best leadership experiences that we read and listened to revealed similar patterns of action. We found that when leaders were at their personal best, they were:

1. Challenging the Process

2. Inspiring a Shared Vision

3. Enabling Others to Act

4. Modeling the Way

5. Encouraging the Heart

In the following paragraphs we've provided brief descriptions of these five practices. You'll find more information in Chapter 7.[2]

CHALLENGING THE PROCESS

Leaders *search for opportunities* to change the status quo. They look for innovative ways to improve the organization. In doing so, they *experiment and take risks*. And because leaders know that risk taking involves mistakes and failures, they accept the inevitable disappointments as learning opportunities.

INSPIRING A SHARED VISION

Leaders passionately believe that they can make a difference. They *envision the future*, creating an ideal and unique image of what the organization can become. Through their magnetism and quiet persuasion, leaders *enlist others* in their dreams. They breathe life into their visions and get people to see exciting possibilities for the future.

ENABLING OTHERS TO ACT

Leaders *foster collaboration* and build spirited teams. They actively involve others. Leaders understand that mutual respect is what sustains extraordinary efforts; they strive to create an atmosphere of trust and human dignity. They *strengthen others*, making each person feel capable and powerful.

MODELING THE WAY

Leaders establish principles concerning the way people (constituents, coworkers, colleagues, and customers alike) should be treated and the way goals should be pursued. They create standards of excellence and then *set an example* for others to follow. Because the prospect of complex change can overwhelm people and stifle action, they set interim goals so that people can *achieve small wins* as they work toward larger objectives. They unravel bureaucracy when it impedes action; they put up signposts when people are unsure of where to go or how to get there; and they create opportunities for victory.

ENCOURAGING THE HEART

Accomplishing extraordinary things in organizations is hard work. To keep hope and determination alive, leaders *recognize contributions* that individuals make. In every winning team, the members need to share in the rewards of their efforts, so leaders *celebrate accomplishments*. They make people feel like heroes.

---

[2]*In addition, each practice is discussed at length in our book,* The Leadership Challenge: How to Keep Getting Extraordinary Things Done in Organizations, *published by Jossey-Bass, San Francisco, in 1995.*

CHAPTER 3

What the LPI-IC Measures

The LPI-IC provides you with information about your leadership behavior. It does not measure IQ, personality, style, or general management skills.

We designed the LPI-IC to be used by multiple raters. By completing the LPI-IC, you and several observers can give feedback on your use of the five leadership practices (Challenging the Process, Inspiring a Shared Vision, Enabling Others to Act, Modeling the Way, and Encouraging the Heart). The people selected as observers must be *only those who directly observe you* in a leadership role.

At a minimum, the observers should include your *constituents* (the members of the team that you lead). The observers also may include your immediate manager and your peers (coworkers in your department or unit). You may even want to include key customers, suppliers, vendors, or managers in other departments. Before you distribute the LPI-IC Observer forms, here are some things you need to do:

1. Write your name on each observer form *in two places:* in the blank marked "Name of Leader" on the front page *and* in the same blank on the response sheet.

2. Check the appropriate box indicating each observer's relationship to you. *Do not write the observers' names on the response sheets.* There are boxes for Constituent, Manager, Peer, and Other. If you are including observers who don't fit in the constituent, manager, or peer categories, check the Other box for these observers.

You'll complete the LPI-IC: Self, and the observers you choose will complete the LPI-IC: Observer. Both you and the observers will indicate how frequently you engage in each of thirty behaviors (six for each leadership practice). The inventory uses a ten-point frequency scale, where "1" indicates "almost never" and "10" indicates "almost always."

WHAT DIFFERENCE DOES THE LPI-IC MAKE?

At this point you may be wondering "Do my scores on the LPI-IC matter? Will it really make a difference if I use the LPI-IC behaviors more often?" Although there are no universal, "right" answers when it comes to leadership, our research consistently shows the same result: *The more frequently you demonstrate the behaviors included in the LPI-IC, the more likely you will be seen as an effective leader.* Figure 1 offers more specific information on how people are perceived when they use LPI-IC behaviors frequently.

People who frequently demonstrate LPI behaviors are seen as:

- Being more effective in meeting job-related demands

- Being more successful in representing their teams to upper management

- Creating higher-performing teams

- Fostering loyalty and commitment

- Increasing motivational levels and willingness to work hard

- Possessing high degrees of personal credibility

FIGURE 1. Observers' Perceptions of People
Who Frequently Use LPI-IC Behaviors

CAN YOU COUNT ON THE LPI-IC FEEDBACK?

Any good instrument should have sound psychometric properties—reliability and validity. In general, an instrument is "reliable" when it measures what it's supposed to measure; it's "valid" when it accurately predicts performance. When we were developing the LPI-IC, we conducted a number of tests to determine whether the inventory had sound psychometric properties. Here's what we found:

The LPI-IC is internally reliable. This means that the six statements pertaining to each leadership practice are highly correlated with one another.

Test-retest reliability is high. This means that scores from one administration of the LPI-IC to another within a short time span (a few months) and without any significant intervening event (such as a leadership-training program) are consistent and stable.

The five scales are generally independent (statistically orthogonal). This means that the five scales—corresponding to the five leadership practices—don't all measure the same phenomenon. Instead, they measure five *different* practices, as they should.

The LPI-IC has both face validity and predictive validity. "Face validity" means that the results make sense to people. "Predictive validity" means that the results are significantly correlated with various performance measures and can be used to make predictions about leadership effectiveness.

SHOULD YOUR SELF AND OBSERVER SCORES BE THE SAME?

Research indicates that trust in a leader is essential if other people are going to follow that person over time. One of the ways that trust is developed is through consistency in leader behavior. Therefore, the closer your view of yourself to the view others have of you, the more likely it is that others will trust you. In the ideal scenario, your self ratings would be consistent with your observer ratings.

In the real world, however, scores aren't always consistent. People may see you differently from the way you see yourself, and they also may differ among themselves as to how they see you. Here are just a few of the possible reasons for such discrepancies:

- Some people may not work with you face to face as often as others; therefore, they may rate you differently on the same behavior.

- Some people may not know you as well as others.

- You may really behave differently in different situations.

- People may differ in their expectations of you.

- Some people may attribute different meanings to the frequency terms used in the LPI-IC. (For example, just how often is "fairly often"?)

The key issue is not whether your self and observer ratings are exactly the same, but whether people perceive consistency between what you say you do and what you actually do. The only way you can know whether that consistency exists is to elicit feedback, and one of the best ways to get that feedback is to use the LPI-IC. Once you have pinpointed any inconsistencies, you can do something about them.

NOW WHAT DO YOU DO WITH THIS INFORMATION?

Feedback is useless unless you act on it. Consider this analogy: If your gas gauge tells you that your car is on empty and you keep driving until your car stalls in the middle of a freeway, is your gas gauge of any use? The LPI-IC is like your gas gauge. It gives you accurate information, but you're the one who has to decide what to do with that information.

As mentioned before, we know from research that leadership consists of observable and learnable behaviors. Even if you've had a great deal of experience in leading others, you can improve your ability to lead if you:

- Receive feedback on your present use of the desired behaviors

- Observe positive models of those behaviors

- Set goals for yourself

- Practice the behaviors

- Ask for and receive updated feedback on your performance

- Set new goals

Of course, there's one more critical ingredient for self-improvement: *desire*. In order to get the most from your LPI-IC feedback, you have to want to improve. It's a good idea to do an internal check to make sure you truly aspire to become a better leader than you are today.

CHAPTER 4

How to Analyze and Interpret LPI-IC Feedback[3]

The purpose of Chapter 4 is to guide you through the process of analyzing a computer-generated LPI-IC feedback report. After you review this chapter, you'll understand how the LPI-IC results are organized and displayed, and you'll be prepared to interpret your own feedback.

Your report will consist of a cover page plus fourteen pages of tables and graphs that present your self and observer ratings on all thirty LPI-IC statements. In this chapter you'll find samples of six of those pages:

1. Summary page

2. Summary graph page

3. Percentile ranking page

4. LPI-IC behaviors ranking page

5. Individual-practice page for Challenging the Process

6. Individual-practice graph page for Challenging the Process

These six sample pages will show you how to read your entire report. They've been completed with a hypothetical leader's results, and we've provided a detailed explanation of the content of each page.

---

[3]*This chapter assumes that your LPI-IC: Self and LPI-IC: Observer forms have been computer scored and that you will receive a computer-generated report of your scores. If this isn't the case, you'll need to record self and observer scores on the grids provided in Appendix B. Even if you won't be receiving a computer-generated report, the practice feedback analysis in this chapter will help you to understand your scores.*

First let's take a look at the summary page (Figure 2).

SUMMARY PAGE

Five Practices

The first or far-left column of the summary page lists the names of the five practices. Although we described the five practices earlier in the sequence of Challenging the Process, Inspiring a Shared Vision, Enabling Others to Act, Modeling the Way, and Encouraging the Heart, you'll notice that on the summary page the practices are displayed in the order of highest to lowest average observer scores.

We've designed the page in this way so that you can quickly find the areas that observers perceive to be your strengths as well as the areas they perceive to be your opportunities for improvement. This information will prove useful later in the LPI-IC feedback process, as you begin to make self-development plans.

Self Rating

The scores in the "Self Rating" column represent the sum of your LPI-IC: Self responses to the six statements about each of the five leadership practices. The score for each practice can range from a high of 60 to a low of 6.

LPI-IC: Observer Ratings

Under the heading "LPI-IC: Observer Ratings" are several columns of scores:

"AVG" (average). The numbers in this column are the averages—practice by practice—of all of the observers' ratings. The average can range from a high of 60 to a low of 6.

```
          LEADERSHIP PRACTICES INVENTORY - INDIVIDUAL CONTRIBUTOR
                        Profile for Jane Doe

              SELF
              RATING    LPI-IC: OBSERVER RATINGS

                        AVG   AGR   M   C1  C2  P1  P2  O1  O2
MODELING
THE WAY         52      50.6   H   51  50  50  50  51  51  51

ENABLING
OTHERS TO ACT   38      47.3   L   43  47  50  50  52  45  44

CHALLENGING
THE PROCESS     43      44.1   L   39  45  45  43  47  46  44

ENCOURAGING
THE HEART       48      44.0   L   46  39  44  42  46  46  45

INSPIRING A
SHARED VISION   44      33.1   M   32  32  33  35  34  33  33


    AVG = Average of all LPI-IC: Observer ratings

    AGR = Degree of consistency between observer scores, with H = High,
          M = Moderate, and L = Low degree of consistency or agreement

  M = Manager      C = Constituent
  P = Peer         O = Other
```

FIGURE 2. Sample Summary Page

"M" (your manager), "C" (constituent), "P" (peer), and "O" (other).
The observer feedback you receive isn't identified by the names of the people who generated it. But these columns tell you what categories the observers were assigned to and how many people were in each category.

The sample summary page has data in all possible observer columns. But when you receive your report, you may or may not have all columns, depending on several factors:

- Whether all categories of observers completed an LPI-IC: Observer form for you

- Whether you wanted observer feedback from people who simply didn't fit in the "M," "C," or "P" categories

- Whether the numbers of observers are large enough to separate into categories (minimum of two observers per category—with the exception of your manager—to protect the observers' anonymity)

- Whether you wanted your observer data separated into categories

For example, let's assume that you gave LPI-IC: Observer forms only to your constituents and you marked the "Constituent" box on every observer response sheet. In this case you'll have feedback from C1, C2, C3, and so on, but you won't have feedback from your manager or other observers.

In another case, let's say that you wanted feedback from your constituents and your manager, but you also wanted feedback from a couple of key customers who observe you frequently in your leadership role. The feedback from those customers wouldn't be appropriate for the "C," "M," or "P" categories, so it will be reported in the "O" columns.

Now let's assume that you gave an observer form to only one peer and you marked the appropriate box for that person. You still won't have peer feedback, because the minimum number of people per category wasn't met. Instead, the data from that one peer will be reported in the "O" columns.

You may even have decided at the outset that you didn't want your observer data separated into categories. In this case all of your data will be reported in the "O" columns.

As you can see, the "O" (Other) designation can function either as a catchall or a default category.

If your summary page doesn't have data from all categories of observers, the other portions of your feedback report also won't have such data.

The codes for individual observers are consistent throughout your report: C1 is always the same person, C2 is always the same person, and so on. The numbers that appear in each column below the category heading on the summary page are the scores per practice for that observer. Again, a score can range from a high of 60 to a low of 6.

SUMMARY GRAPH PAGE

Next look at Figure 3, a printout page that consists of bar graphs. In this sample we've shown bar graphs only for Modeling the Way. But this page in your report will have a set of bar graphs for each of the five practices, listed in the order of highest to lowest average observer scores. The corresponding numerical scores appear in the right column. Self bars and scores are displayed first, followed by bars and scores for observers. Each observer bar represents the *average* score for that category, so the set of bars for each practice illustrates how the different categories of scores compare.

```
                 LEADERSHIP PRACTICES INVENTORY - INDIVIDUAL CONTRIBUTOR
                                 Profile for Jane Doe
MODELING THE WAY

        Self         ========================================         52.0
        Manager      =======================================          51.0
        Constituents ======================================           50.0
        Peers        ========================================         50.5
        Others       =======================================          51.0


ENABLING OTHERS TO ACT

        Self
        Manager
        Constituents
        Peers
        Others


CHALLENGING THE PROCESS

        Self
        Manager
        Constituents
        Peers
        Others


ENCOURAGING THE HEART

        Self
        Manager
        Constituents
        Peers
        Others


INSPIRING A SHARED VISION

        Self
        Manager
        Constituents
        Peers
        Others
```

FIGURE 3. Sample Summary Graph Page

In Figure 3 there are bars for all possible sources of data: self, constituents, manager, peers, and others. When you receive your report, you may or may not have all of these bars, depending on whether your observers have been divided into categories and which categories you have.

Interpreting the Summary Information

Take a few moments to study the sample summary—both the numerical ratings in Figure 2 and the bar graphs in Figure 3—and analyze the hypothetical leader's feedback. Think about how you would answer these questions:

1. How does the leader rate herself? In which practice does she give herself the highest rating? The second? Third? Fourth? The lowest rating? These ratings indicate areas that she considers to be her strengths and areas in which she might consider improvement.

2. In which practice do the observers give her the highest rating? The second? Third? Fourth? The lowest rating? These ratings indicate what the observers, on average, consider to be her strengths and areas for improvement.

3. What similarities do you find in the self and average observer ratings with regard to strengths and areas for improvement? What differences do you find? What factors might explain the differences?

4. Look at the numerical ratings given by *individual observers*. How does the leader's manager rate her? Compare the individual constituents to one another, the individual peers to one another, and the individual other observers to one another. Do the people in each of these observer categories generally agree or disagree with one another? What are the similarities within each category? What are the differences? What might account for the differences?

5. Analyze the numerical ratings and bar charts by *categories*. Compare the self, manager, average constituent, average peer, and average other-observer ratings to one another. What areas of agreement and disagreement do you find? What might you conclude from your findings?

PERCENTILE RANKING PAGE

Figure 4 is a sample of the page that compares your scores to those of all people in the LPI-IC database. The percentile rankings have been determined by the percentage of those people who have scored at or below a given number. For example, let's say that your score for Challenging the Process is at the 70th percentile line. This means that you scored higher in that practice than 70 percent of all of the people who have taken the LPI-IC. In other words, you are in the top 30 percent for Challenging the Process.

The numbers along the left margin in Figure 4 represent percentile rankings in increments of ten. We've divided the graph into three segments with horizontal lines, representing the top, middle, and bottom third of the scores. From left to right are columns for Challenging, Inspiring, Enabling, Modeling, and Encouraging. Your own percentile rankings for these practices will be plotted on the graph and connected with lines.

Here's what the different lines illustrate: "S" = self ratings, "M" = your manager's rating, "C" = average rating for constituents, "P" = average rating for peers, "O" = average rating for other observers.

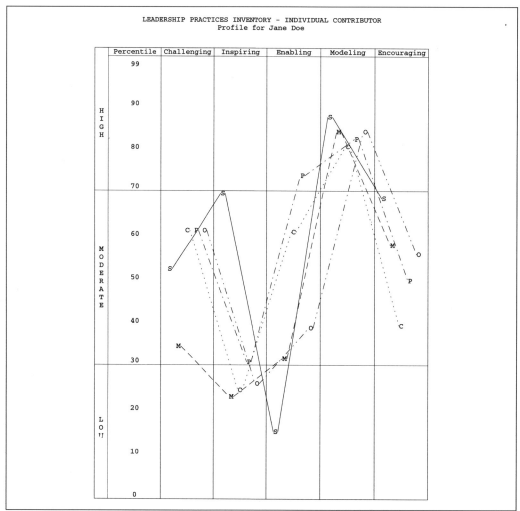

FIGURE 4. Sample Percentile Ranking Page

Your own percentile ranking page may be different. If you don't have observer categories, you'll see two lines: (1) one marked "S" for self and (2) one marked "O," representing responses from all of the people who completed LPI-IC: Observer forms for you.

Essentially, the percentile rankings are benchmarking numbers that provide a context for your scores. Our studies indicate that a "high" score is one at the 70th percentile or above, whereas a "low" score is one at the 30th percentile or below. A score that falls between 31 and 69 percent would be considered "moderate."

Analyzing the Percentile Ranking Page

Let's examine the hypothetical leader's percentile rankings in Figure 4 and see what they reveal. Think about how you would answer the following questions:

1. First look at the leader's self scores, designated by the line marked "S." In which percentile does each of the five practices fall? How do her percentiles compare with those of others in the LPI-IC database? In which areas does she believe she's strong? In which areas does she believe there's room for improvement?

2. Next look at the scores from the leader's manager, designated by the line marked "M." What are the percentiles for each of the five practices? How do these percentiles compare with those in the LPI-IC database? What does the leader's manager consider to be her strengths? What does the manager consider to be her opportunities for improvement?

3. Now look at the remaining scores: the constituents' (the line marked "C"), the peers' (the line marked "P"), and the other observers' (the line marked "O"). How do these ratings compare with those in the LPI-IC database? What do these different categories of observers believe to be the leader's strengths? What do they believe to be areas in which she needs to improve?

4. Compare the self line with the lines for the different categories of observers. Are they parallel or do they intersect? If the lines are parallel, then the leader and the different categories of observers basically agree about her strengths and opportunities for improvement. If the lines intersect, then the leader and the observers disagree. In the case of this leader, where is there agreement? Where is there disagreement?

5. Look at the degrees of distance between the self line and the different observer lines. These distances illustrate the areas of agreement and disagreement between self and observers. Are this leader's self and observer lines close together or far apart? Where are there similar scores? Where are the differences most pronounced?

LPI-IC BEHAVIORS RANKING PAGE

Figure 5 is a sample of the LPI-IC behaviors ranking page. This page displays ratings for each of the thirty behavioral statements, which are listed in abbreviated form.

The statements are ranked in order from highest to lowest average observer score. In addition, there's a horizontal line isolating the ten lowest scores.

For purposes of comparison, the self ratings are displayed next to the average observer ratings. A score marked with an *asterisk* (*) indicates that the average observer score and the self score differ by more than plus or minus 1.5.

```
              LEADERSHIP PRACTICES INVENTORY - INDIVIDUAL CONTRIBUTOR
                             Profile for Jane Doe

                 Leadership Behaviors Ranked by LPI-IC: Observer Scores

                                                              SELF  OBSERVERS

      9. Ensures that people adhere to agreed-on standards  MODELING      9    8.7
     19. Is clear about meaning of "doing one's best"       MODELING      9    8.7
     14. Follows through on promises and commitments         MODELING      8    8.6
     16. Asks "What can we learn"?                           CHALLENGING   7    8.6 *
     24. Helps ensure that goals, plans, milestones are set  MODELING      8    8.4
      3. Develops cooperative relationships                  ENABLING      6    8.1 *
     29. Makes progress toward goals one step at a time      MODELING      9    8.1
      4. Sets example of what is expected                    MODELING      9    8.0
      8. Listens to diverse points of view                  ENABLING      6    8.0 *
     23. Gives others freedom in making decisions            ENABLING      8    8.0
     28. Helps people learn and develop in their work        ENABLING      3    7.9 *
     18. Supports other people's decisions                   ENABLING      8    7.7
     13. Treats people with dignity and respect              ENABLING      7    7.6
     15. Creatively rewards people for their contributions   ENCOURAGING   8    7.6
      5. Praises people for a job well done                  ENCOURAGING   7    7.4
     10. Expresses confidence in people's abilities          ENCOURAGING   8    7.4
     30. Gives team members appreciation and support         ENCOURAGING  10    7.4 *
     21. Experiments and takes risks                         CHALLENGING   7    7.3
     25. Finds ways to celebrate accomplishments             ENCOURAGING   7    7.3
      1. Seeks challenging opportunities                     CHALLENGING   6    7.1
     ─────────────────────────────────────────────────────────────────────────
      6. Challenges people to try new approaches             CHALLENGING   7    7.1
     11. Looks outside organization for ways to improve      CHALLENGING   9    7.1 *
     20. Recognizes people for commitment to shared values   ENCOURAGING   8    6.9
     26. Takes initiative to overcome obstacles              CHALLENGING   7    6.9
     17. Shows others how the vision is in their interests   INSPIRING     8    5.9 *
     27. Speaks with conviction about meaning of work        INSPIRING     6    5.9
      7. Describes compelling image of future                INSPIRING     7    5.6
     22. Is enthusiastic and positive about future           INSPIRING     8    5.4 *
     12. Appeals to others to share dream of future          INSPIRING     8    5.3 *
      2. Talks about future trends                           INSPIRING     7    5.1 *


   * Difference between Observers' and Self rating was greater than 1.5


   1       2       3         4          5           6         7       8         9         10
   |-------|-------|---------|----------|-----------|---------|-------|---------|---------|
   Almost  Rarely  Seldom    Once       Occasionally Sometimes Fairly Usually   Very      Almost
   Never                     in a While                         Often          Frequently Always
```

FIGURE 5. Sample LPI-IC Behaviors Ranking Page

The thirty LPI-IC statements specify behaviors that, according to our research, exemplify the five practices. The practice to which each statement applies is listed on the LPI-IC behaviors ranking page. The feedback on specific behaviors will help you decide how to target your improvement efforts and how to build on your strengths. Also, you'll want to review your scores from time to time, and this page can serve as a quick reference for that purpose.

The numbers in the "Self" and "Observers" columns on the right can range from 10.0 to 1.0, because each behavior was rated on a frequency scale from 10 to 1:

10 = Almost Always
9 = Very Frequently
8 = Usually
7 = Fairly Often
6 = Sometimes
5 = Occasionally
4 = Once in a While
3 = Seldom
2 = Rarely
1 = Almost Never

Interpreting the LPI-IC Behaviors Ranking Page

Let's analyze the LPI-IC behaviors ranking page for our hypothetical leader. How would you answer the following questions?

1. First look at the highest-rated items in Figure 5. Which specific leadership behaviors does this leader exhibit most often? These behaviors are her strengths.

2. Next look at the lowest-rated items. The ten behaviors that this leader exhibits least often are listed below the horizontal line. Which behaviors are they? These behaviors represent opportunities for improvement, regardless of their scores.

3. Do you see items from one practice that form a cluster? If three or more items form a cluster at the lower end of the scale, then it's important to pay attention to that practice as a whole rather than just as single behaviors.

4. Which items are marked with an asterisk (*)? These items warrant further investigation to find out why agreement between self and observers is so low.

5. What conclusions can you draw from this LPI-IC behaviors ranking page? Given the information on this page, where would you suggest that the leader begin her development planning?

INDIVIDUAL-PRACTICE PAGE FOR CHALLENGING THE PROCESS

The LPI-IC feedback report includes two pages for *each* of the five leadership practices. These pages, the individual-practice page and the individual-practice graph page, follow the formats of the summary page and the summary graph page, respectively. We've included samples illustrating the hypothetical leader's results for Challenging the Process. Let's look at the first of the two pages, the individual-practice page (Figure 6), and see what it tells us.

```
              LEADERSHIP PRACTICES INVENTORY - INDIVIDUAL CONTRIBUTOR
                            CHALLENGING THE PROCESS

                              Profile for Jane Doe

LEADERSHIP                        SELF
BEHAVIOR                          RATING   LPI-IC: OBSERVER RATINGS

                                           AVG   M   C1  C2  P1  P2  O1  O2

16. Asks "What can we               7       8.6   9  10   9   8   9   8   7
    learn"?

21. Experiments and takes           7       7.3   3   8   8   7   9   8   8
    risks

 1. Seeks challenging               6       7.1   7   7   7   7   7   7   8
    opportunities

 6. Challenges people to            7       7.1   8   6   7   7   8   7   7
    try new approaches

11. Looks outside organization     9       7.1   7   8   7   7   7   8   6
    for ways to improve

26. Takes initiative to             7       6.9   5   6   7   7   7   8   8
    overcome obstacles


CUMULATIVE RATINGS:                43      44.1  39  45  45  43  47  46  44


  1        2        3         4           5            6          7        8          9           10
  |-- ---|-------|---------|------------|------------|---------|-------|---------|----------|
Almost  Rarely  Seldom    Once       Occasionally  Sometimes Fairly Usually    Very      Almost
Never                   in a While                            Often           Frequently  Always
```

FIGURE 6. Sample Individual-Practice Page for Challenging the Process

Leadership Behavior

The first or far-left column is labeled "Leadership Behavior." Each numbered item in this column is an abbreviated form of an LPI-IC statement related to the practice. As you can see in Figure 6, items 1, 6, 11, 16, 21, and 26 relate to Challenging the Process.

On each individual-practice page, the abbreviated statements are listed in the order of highest to lowest average observer scores. This order of display gives you a quick look at the behaviors that others perceive to be your greatest strengths and your greatest opportunities for improvement within that particular practice—information that you'll need when you're making self-development plans.

Self Rating

The numbers in the "Self Rating" column are the scores you gave yourself for the individual items. Because the rating scale ranges from a high of 10 to a low of 1, your individual scores can range from 10 to 1.

LPI-IC Observer Ratings

As is the case with the summary page, several types of observer scores are listed in the "LPI-IC Observer Ratings" column:

"AVG" (average). The numbers in this column, which can range from 10 to 1, are the item-by-item averages of all of the observers' ratings.

"M" (your manager), "C" (constituent), "P" (peer), and "O" (other). The observer feedback on the individual-practice page, like that on the summary page, is identified by category and tells you how many people in each category submitted an LPI-IC Observer form.

As is the case with the sample summary page, the sample individual-practice page has data in all possible observer columns. But your own individual-practice pages may or may not have all of this data, depending on your circumstances.

Keep in mind that the codes for individual observers are consistent throughout your feedback report. C1, for example, on each individual-practice page is the same person designated as C1 on your summary page. Again, a single observer score can range from 10 to 1.

INDIVIDUAL-PRACTICE GRAPH PAGE
FOR CHALLENGING THE PROCESS

Figure 7 is a sample of the second of the two feedback pages for each practice, the individual-practice graph page. This page displays a set of bar graphs and corresponding numerical scores for each of the six statements that pertain to that practice. The statements are listed in order of highest to lowest average observer score.

Self bars and scores appear first, followed by observer bars and average scores. Again, your report may not reflect some types of observer data.

```
          LEADERSHIP PRACTICES INVENTORY - INDIVIDUAL CONTRIBUTOR
                        CHALLENGING THE PROCESS

                          Profile for Jane Doe

16: I ask "What did we learn from this experience?" when things do not go as
    expected:

      Self          ===================================        7.0
      Manager       ==========================================  9.0
      Constituents  ============================================ 9.5
      Peers         ========================================    8.5
      Others        =============================              7.5


21: I experiment and take risks even when there is a chance of failure:

      Self          ================================          7.0
      Manager       ===============                           3.0
      Constituents  =====================================     8.0
      Peers         =====================================     8.0
      Others        =====================================     8.0


 1: I provide opportunites for people to challenge themselves by trying out new
    ways of doing things:

      Self          ============================              6.0
      Manager       ===============================           7.0
      Constituents  ===============================           7.0
      Peers         ===============================           7.0
      Others        ===================================       7.5


 6: I seek out challenging opportunities that test my own skills and abilities:

      Self          ================================          7.0
      Manager       ====================================      8.0
      Constituents  =============================             6.5
      Peers         ==================================        7.5
      Others        ================================          7.0


11: I search outside the formal boundaries of my organization for innovative ways
    to improve what we do:

      Self          ==========================================  9.0
      Manager       =================================          7.0
      Constituents  ====================================       7.5
      Peers         ===============================            7.0
      Others        ===============================            7.0


26: I take initiative to overcome obstacles even when outcomes are uncertain:

      Self          ================================          7.0
      Manager       ==========================                5.0
      Constituents  ============================              6.5
      Peers         ================================          7.0
      Others        =====================================     8.0
```

FIGURE 7. Sample Individual-Practice Graph Page for Challenging the Process

Interpreting the Sample Pages for Challenging the Process

Let's examine both sample pages (Figures 6 and 7) and see what we can determine about the hypothetical leader's use of Challenging the Process. Think about how you would answer these questions:

1. How does this leader rate herself on the six items? On which item does she give herself the first or highest rating? The second? Third? Fourth? Fifth? The lowest rating? These ratings indicate her own opinions about the areas that are her strengths and the areas that represent opportunities for improvement.

2. On average, how do the observers rate her? What item has the highest rating? The second? Third? Fourth? Fifth? The lowest rating?

3. Are the self and average observer ratings similar? Where are there differences in perception? What might explain the differences?

4. Examine the ratings given by *individual observers*. How does the leader's manager rate her? Also compare the individual constituents to one another, the individual peers to one another, and the individual other observers to one another. Do the people in each of these observer categories generally agree or disagree with one another? What are the similarities within each category? What are the differences? What might account for the differences?

5. Analyze the numerical ratings and bar charts by *categories*. Compare the self, manager, average constituent, average peer, and average other-observer ratings to one another. What areas of agreement and disagreement do you find? What might you conclude from your findings?

CHAPTER 5

Interpreting Your Own LPI-IC Feedback[4]

Now that you've practiced analyzing a hypothetical leader's LPI-IC feedback, you're ready to analyze and interpret your own feedback report. As explained in Chapter 4, you may or may not have scores from all categories of observers, depending on several factors. And if your observers were not divided into categories, your report will have only self ("S") and other ("O") information. When you find questions in this chapter dealing with observer categories that you don't have, ignore them.

Keep in mind that you'll be using your analysis of the feedback (your answers to the questions in this chapter) as a foundation for your self-development plans. As a result, in addition to answering the questions, you should jot down notes about any additional information you'd like to have from observers. If you have time, you might also want to make brief notes about additional conclusions you can draw, issues or implications you should consider, and actions you might consider taking.

First you'll work through the data pertaining to your overall feedback. Then you'll go through the five individual practices one by one.

---

[4]*This chapter assumes that you have received a computer-generated LPI-IC feedback report. If this isn't the case and you haven't yet scored your LPI-IC: Self and LPI-IC: Observer forms, turn to Appendix B and follow the instructions for scoring. Then work through this chapter, answering as many questions as you can.*

YOUR SUMMARY PAGE AND
SUMMARY GRAPH PAGE

Open your feedback report to the two pages that summarize your scores: the summary page and the summary graph page. Examine the feedback and write answers in the spaces provided.

1. First look at the ratings you gave yourself.

   • In which practice do you have the highest rating?

   • The second?

   • Third?

   • Fourth?

   • Fifth?

   • According to the ratings you gave yourself, what are your strengths?

   • According to your self ratings, what are the areas in which you might consider making improvements?

2. Now look at the average observer ratings.

  • In which practice did the observers give you the highest rating?

  • The second?

  • Third?

  • Fourth?

  • Fifth?

  • What do the observers indicate are your strengths?

  • What do the observers indicate are areas in which you need to improve?

3. Next compare the ratings you gave yourself to the average observer ratings.

- Do you and the observers perceive your strengths to be the same or different? Where are the similarities and differences? What might explain the differences?

- What about the areas in which you need to improve? Do you and the observers have the same or different perceptions? Where are the similarities and differences? What might explain the differences?

4. Examine the numerical ratings given by *individual observers*.

• How did your manager rate you for each practice?

• Compare the individual constituents (C1, C2, etc.) to one another, the individual peers (P1, P2, etc.) to one another, and the individual other observers (O1, O2, etc.) to one another. *(If you don't have separate observer categories, just compare your observers—O1, O2, etc.—to one another.)* In each category, where is there agreement *among the individuals?*

• Where is there disagreement?

• What can you conclude from this information?

5. Analyze the numerical ratings and bar charts by *categories*. Compare the self, manager, average constituent, average peer, and average other-observer ratings to one another. *(If you don't have separate observer categories, skip this item.)*

• What are the similarities *between categories?*

• What are the differences?

• What can you conclude from your findings? Consider the information, for example, in terms of who's closest to you: Do your manager and your constituents tend to be in greater agreement than the other observers, whose relationships may be more distant?

YOUR PERCENTILE RANKING PAGE

Open your feedback report to the percentile ranking page. This is the page that offers you a way of benchmarking yourself against a cross-section of the leadership population—all of the people who make up the LPI-IC database.

The "S" line illustrates the scores you gave yourself. If you have scores from all categories of observers, you'll have lines marked "M" for manager, "C" for constituents, "P" for peers, and "O" for other observers. If you don't have observer categories, you'll see two lines: (1) one marked "S" for self and (2) one marked "O," representing responses from all of the people who completed LPI-IC: Observer forms for you.

Examine the page and write answers to the following questions:

1. First look at the "S" line illustrating the ratings you gave yourself.

- In which percentile does each practice fall?

Challenging	Inspiring	Enabling	Modeling	Encouraging
_____	_____	_____	_____	_____

- In which areas are your self ratings strong, compared to others in the database?

- In which areas do your self ratings indicate that you have greater opportunities for improvement than others in the database?

- How does this information compare to what you learned about your self ratings from the summary page and the summary graph page? Are there any surprises? If so, what are they?

2. Now look at the lines designating the observer scores.

- In which percentiles are your scores for each observer category? *(If you don't have separate observer categories, record the percentiles for all observers in the row marked "O.")*

	Challenging	Inspiring	Enabling	Modeling	Encouraging
M (Manager)	_____	_____	_____	_____	_____
C (Constituents)	_____	_____	_____	_____	_____
P (Peers)	_____	_____	_____	_____	_____
O (Other Observers)	_____	_____	_____	_____	_____

- Where is there agreement among the observer categories about your strengths and opportunities for improvement, compared to people in the LPI-IC database?

- Where is there disagreement?

- What does this information indicate to you?

3. Compare your self line to your observer lines.

- Are they parallel or do they intersect?

- Are they close together or far apart?

- Where are the greatest differences?

- Would you say, in general, that you *are* or *are not* in agreement with the observers?

YOUR LPI-IC BEHAVIORS RANKING PAGE

Open your feedback report to the LPI-IC behaviors ranking page. Remember that on this page the items, which are abbreviations of the statements in the LPI-IC, are ranked in order according to average observer rating. Read the feedback carefully and answer the following questions:

1. First look at the highest-ranked items (your strengths). Which specific behaviors are they?

2. Now look at the lowest-ranked items (your opportunities for improvement).

   • Which specific behaviors are they?

   • Examine the lowest-ranked items to see whether you have three or more from one practice. If so, then you need to pay attention to that practice as a whole, rather than just as individual behaviors. Is this the case for you? If so, which practice is involved?

3. Compare your self ratings to the average observer ratings.

- In general, would you say that they're in agreement?

- Look at any items marked with an asterisk (*). The asterisk indicates that the self score and the average observer score differ by more than plus or minus 1.5. In other words, agreement between self and observers is low. Which items on your page are marked with an asterisk? (Later you'll want to look at the more detailed item feedback for each practice to gain a better understanding of any sources of low agreement.)

4. Given the data on this page, consider how you might approach your development planning. Where would you begin? With which practice?

YOUR FEEDBACK FOR
CHALLENGING THE PROCESS

Open your feedback report to the two pages on Challenging the Process. Review your feedback and answer the questions following the boxed statements. *(Skip questions as necessary if you don't have certain categories of observers.)*

The Six LPI-IC Statements for Challenging the Process

1. I seek out challenging opportunities that test my own skills and abilities.

6. I challenge people to try out new and innovative approaches to their work.

11. I search outside the formal boundaries of my organization for innovative ways to improve what we do.

16. I ask "What can we learn?" when things do not go as expected.

21. I experiment and take risks in my work even when there is a chance of failure.

26. I take the initiative to overcome obstacles even when outcomes are uncertain.

I. Self Ratings

• For which behavior do you have the highest rating?

• The second?

• Third?

• Fourth?

• Fifth?

• Sixth?

• According to your self ratings, which behaviors are your strengths?

• Which behaviors warrant improvement?

2. Average Observer Ratings

• For which behavior did the observers give you the highest rating?

• The second?

• Third?

• Fourth?

• Fifth?

• Sixth?

• Which behaviors do observers indicate are your strengths?

• Which do they indicate are opportunities for improvement?

3. Comparison of Self Ratings to Average Observer Ratings

• What are the similarities?

• What are the differences? What might explain them?

4. Analysis of Individual Observer Ratings

- How does your manager rate you in each of the six behaviors?

- Compare the individual constituents to one another, the individual peers to one another, and the individual other observers to one another. What are the similarities *within each category?*

- What are the differences? What might account for them?

5. Analysis of Ratings and Bar Charts by Categories

- Compare the self, manager, average constituent, average peer, and average other-observer ratings to one another. Where do you see similarities *between categories?*

- Where do you see differences?

- What can you conclude from your findings?

YOUR FEEDBACK FOR
INSPIRING A SHARED VISION

Open your feedback report to the two pages on Inspiring a Shared Vision. Review your feedback and answer the questions following the boxed statements. *(Skip questions as necessary if you don't have certain categories of observers.)*

The Six LPI-IC Statements for Inspiring a Shared Vision

2. I talk about future trends that will influence how our work gets done.

7. I describe a compelling image of what our future could be like.

12. I appeal to others to share in my dream of future possibilities.

17. I show others how it is in their long-term interests to work together on a common vision.

22. I am contagiously enthusiastic and positive about future possibilities.

27. I speak with genuine conviction about the higher meaning and purpose of our work.

---

1. Self Ratings

- For which behavior do you have the highest rating?

- The second?

- Third?

- Fourth?

- Fifth?

- Sixth?

• According to your self ratings, which behaviors are your strengths?

• Which behaviors warrant improvement?

2. Average Observer Ratings

• For which behavior did the observers give you the highest rating?

• The second?

• Third?

• Fourth?

• Fifth?

• Sixth?

• Which behaviors do observers indicate are your strengths?

• Which do they indicate are opportunities for improvement?

3. Comparison of Self Ratings to Average Observer Ratings

• What are the similarities?

• What are the differences? What might explain them?

4. Analysis of Individual Observer Ratings

- How does your manager rate you in each of the six behaviors?

- Compare the individual constituents to one another, the individual peers to one another, and the individual other observers to one another. What are the similarities *within each category?*

- What are the differences? What might account for them?

5. Analysis of Ratings and Bar Charts by Categories

- Compare the self, manager, average constituent, average peer, and average other-observer ratings to one another. Where do you see similarities *between categories?*

- Where do you see differences?

- What can you conclude from your findings?

YOUR FEEDBACK FOR
ENABLING OTHERS TO ACT

Open your feedback report to the two pages on Enabling Others to Act. Review your feedback and answer the questions following the boxed statements. *(Skip questions as necessary if you don't have certain categories of observers.)*

The Six LPI-IC Statements for Enabling Others to Act

3. I develop cooperative relationships among the people I work with.

8. I actively listen to diverse points of view.

13. I treat others with dignity and respect.

18. I support the decisions that people make on their own.

23. I give others freedom and choice in making decisions about issues that affect them.

28. I take an active role in helping people learn and develop in their work.

I. Self Ratings

• For which behavior do you have the highest rating?

• The second?

• Third?

• Fourth?

• Fifth?

• Sixth?

• According to your self ratings, which behaviors are your strengths?

• Which behaviors warrant improvement?

2. Average Observer Ratings

• For which behavior did the observers give you the highest rating?

• The second?

• Third?

• Fourth?

• Fifth?

• Sixth?

• Which behaviors do observers indicate are your strengths?

• Which do they indicate are opportunities for improvement?

3. Comparison of Self Ratings to Average Observer Ratings

• What are the similarities?

• What are the differences? What might explain them?

4. Analysis of Individual Observer Ratings

- How does your manager rate you in each of the six behaviors?

- Compare the individual constituents to one another, the individual peers to one another, and the individual other observers to one another. What are the similarities *within each category?*

- What are the differences? What might account for them?

5. Analysis of Ratings and Bar Charts by Categories

- Compare the self, manager, average constituent, average peer, and average other-observer ratings to one another. Where do you see similarities *between categories?*

- Where do you see differences?

- What can you conclude from your findings?

YOUR FEEDBACK FOR MODELING THE WAY

Open your feedback report to the two pages on Modeling the Way. Review your feedback and answer the questions following the boxed statements. *(Skip questions as necessary if you don't have certain categories of observers.)*

The Six LPI-IC Statements for Modeling the Way

4. I set a personal example of what I expect from others.

9. I spend time and energy on making certain that people's actions are consistent with the values and standards that have been agreed on.

14. I follow through on the promises and commitments that I make.

19. I am clear with others about what it means to do one's best.

24. I take an active part in making certain that achievable goals, concrete plans, and measurable milestones are set for the projects and programs that we work on.

29. I make progress toward goals one step at a time.

I. Self Ratings

• For which behavior do you have the highest rating?

• The second?

• Third?

• Fourth?

• Fifth?

• Sixth?

• According to your self ratings, which behaviors are your strengths?

• Which behaviors warrant improvement?

2. Average Observer Ratings

• For which behavior did the observers give you the highest rating?

• The second?

• Third?

• Fourth?

• Fifth?

• Sixth?

• Which behaviors do observers indicate are your strengths?

• Which do they indicate are opportunities for improvement?

3. Comparison of Self Ratings to Average Observer Ratings

• What are the similarities?

• What are the differences? What might explain them?

4. Analysis of Individual Observer Ratings

• How does your manager rate you in each of the six behaviors?

• Compare the individual constituents to one another, the individual peers to one another, and the individual other observers to one another. What are the similarities *within each category?*

• What are the differences? What might account for them?

5. Analysis of Ratings and Bar Charts by Categories

• Compare the self, manager, average constituent, average peer, and average other-observer ratings to one another. Where do you see similarities *between categories?*

• Where do you see differences?

• What can you conclude from your findings?

YOUR FEEDBACK FOR ENCOURAGING THE HEART

Open your feedback report to the two pages on Encouraging the Heart. Review your feedback and answer the questions following the boxed statements. *(Skip questions as necessary if you don't have certain categories of observers.)*

The Six LPI-IC Statements for Encouraging the Heart

5. I praise people for a job well done.

10. I make it a point to let people know about my confidence in their abilities.

15. I make sure that people are creatively rewarded for their contributions to the success of our projects.

20. I publicly recognize people who exemplify commitment to shared values.

25. I find ways to celebrate accomplishments with my team.

30. I give the members of the team lots of appreciation and support for their contributions.

I. Self Ratings

• For which behavior do you have the highest rating?

• The second?

• Third?

• Fourth?

• Fifth?

• Sixth?

• According to your self ratings, which behaviors are your strengths?

• Which behaviors warrant improvement?

2. Average Observer Ratings

• For which behavior did the observers give you the highest rating?

• The second?

• Third?

• Fourth?

• Fifth?

• Sixth?

• Which behaviors do observers indicate are your strengths?

• Which do they indicate are opportunities for improvement?

3. Comparison of Self Ratings to Average Observer Ratings

• What are the similarities?

• What are the differences? What might explain them?

4. Analysis of Individual Observer Ratings

• How does your manager rate you in each of the six behaviors?

• Compare the individual constituents to one another, the individual peers to one another, and the individual other observers to one another. What are the similarities *within each category?*

• What are the differences? What might account for them?

5. Analysis of Ratings and Bar Charts by Categories

• Compare the self, manager, average constituent, average peer, and average other-observer ratings to one another. Where do you see similarities *between categories?*

• Where do you see differences?

• What can you conclude from your findings?

CHAPTER 6

Summarizing Your Feedback

By this time you've analyzed a lot of feedback about your use of the five leadership practices that make up the LPI-IC. Take a few minutes now to review your comments in Chapter 5 and summarize them here so that you can make plans for improvement.

At this point you also need to make choices about where to begin. Don't try to work on all of the practices at once; instead, choose one or two that you most want to work on. Then, once you've completed the summary and made your decision, go to Chapter 7 and read the appropriate lists of suggestions on how to improve in the practice(s) you've chosen.

1. What are your strengths, according to your own analysis?

2. What are your strengths, according to the observers?

3. What are your opportunities for improvement, according to your own analysis?

4. What are your opportunities for improvement, according to the observers?

5. What are the areas of greatest agreement between yourself and the observers?

6. What are the areas of greatest disagreement?

7. Where would you most like to focus your efforts in improving your use of the five leadership practices? Rank order the practices in terms of your development priorities.

_____ Challenging the Process

_____ Inspiring a Shared Vision

_____ Enabling Others to Act

_____ Modeling the Way

_____ Encouraging the Heart

8. Which specific behaviors would you most like to work on?

CHAPTER 7

Continuing Your Leadership Development

With the help of the LPI-IC, you've been given the gift of feedback about your leadership practices. And with the help of this workbook, you've taken a hard look at yourself as a leader. Now it's time to act on the insights you've gained. It's time to start becoming an even-better leader than you are today.

THREE OPPORTUNITIES FOR LEARNING TO LEAD

Just how do you learn to lead? We posed that question in our research, and from an analysis of thousands of responses we identified three major opportunities for learning to lead: trial and error, observation, and education.

The purpose of this chapter is to acquaint you with ways to take advantage of these three opportunities. For each of the five practices, we've provided suggestions for all three opportunities. You'll find them under the headings "Learning by Doing," "Learning from Others," and "Learning in the Classroom or on Your Own." But before you proceed to the ideas for the individual practices, we'd like to offer our perspective on the roles of trial and error, observation, and education in leadership development.

Trial and error: Learning by doing. There's no suitable substitute for learning by doing. Whether it's facilitating meetings, leading a special task force, heading your favorite charity's fund-raising drive, or chairing your professional association's annual conference, the more chances you have to serve in leadership roles, the more likely it is that you'll develop the skills to lead—and the more likely that you'll learn the important leadership lessons that come only from the failures and successes of live action.

Just any experience, however, does not by itself support individual development. Challenge is crucial to learning. Boring, routine jobs don't help you improve your skills and abilities. You must stretch. You must take opportunities to test yourself against new and difficult tasks. So experience can indeed be the best teacher—if it includes the element of personal challenge. Whether you choose activities from our "Learning by Doing" lists or you invent your own, make sure that your selections involve a stretch for you.

Observation: Learning from others. Other people are excellent sources of guidance: parents, teachers, neighbors, coaches, counselors, artisans, friends, coworkers, mentors, managers. Think about the people who've given you advice and support, filled you with curiosity, let you watch them while they worked, believed you had promise and inspired you to give your best, offered feedback about your behavior and its impact, and taught you the ropes.

What you continue to learn from these people and others can help you become a better leader. As you think about your continuing leadership development, look around for role models, coaches, and teachers in your organization or community. Don't be shy about asking for their help or about watching them at work.

And even though you can't observe them directly, well-known contemporary or past leaders are also an excellent source of learning. Pick up a couple of biographies and read how these people became esteemed leaders.

Education: Learning in the classroom or on your own. Formal training can improve your chances of success. According to a study by the American Society for Training and Development (ASTD), ". . .people who are trained formally in the workplace have a 30 percent higher productivity rate after one year than people who are not formally trained."[5]

You should be spending *at least fifty hours annually* on your personal and professional development. At Motorola and Solectron, two companies that have received the Malcolm Baldrige National Quality Award, people spend *one hundred hours* per year! In fact, Baldrige Award-winning companies in general spend about twice as much on training as the U.S. average of 1.4 percent of payroll.[6] If you want to have this kind of success, take a cue from these companies.

For each practice you want to improve, commit to participating in at least one formal workshop or seminar during the next few months. Also consider the possibility of self-directed training—a course that you can complete on your own time and at your own pace. And once you've completed the training, make sure you experiment with the new behaviors you learn. In the final analysis, everything about learning to be an effective leader is dependent on the most important source of continual personal improvement: learning by doing.

Now review the developmental priorities that you listed in Chapter 6, and then turn to the appropriate page in this chapter to find ideas about how to improve your leadership ability: Challenging the Process: page 58, Inspiring a Shared Vision: page 62, Enabling Others to Act: page 66, Modeling the Way: page 70, and Encouraging the Heart: page 74.

---

[5]*From* Put Quality to Work: Train America's Workforce *by A.P. Carnevale, Alexandria, VA: American Society for Training and Development, 1990, p. 11. See also* Accounting for United States Economic Growth 1929–1969 *by E. Denison, Washington, DC: The Brookings Institution, 1988.*

[6]*A.P. Carnevale,* Put Quality to Work: Train America's Workforce, *Alexandria, VA: American Society for Training and Development, 1990, p. 11.*

IMPROVING IN CHALLENGING THE PROCESS

Leaders *search for opportunities* to change the status quo. They look for innovative ways to improve their organizations. They *experiment and take risks.* And because risk taking involves mistakes and failure, leaders accept the inevitable disappointments as learning opportunities.

Following are some suggestions on how to improve in Challenging the Process. Put a check mark next to each one that could work for you. Below each idea you choose, write a brief note about a specific action you could take to implement that idea in your particular situation. Feel free to add ideas of your own.

Learning by Doing

____ Volunteer for a tough assignment in your workplace or your community. Be proactive in looking for chances to stretch yourself and learn something.

____ Treat every day as if it were your first day at work. Accept it as a brand-new challenge. Ask yourself "What can I do today so that I'll do my job better and smarter than yesterday?"

____ Make a list of every task you perform. About each, ask yourself "Why am I doing this? Why am I doing it this way? Can this task be eliminated or done significantly better?"

____ Don't let regular meetings with your constituents become strictly status reports. Devote at least 25 percent of the time to improvement and innovation (of processes, products, services, or whatever).

____ About every policy and procedure that your team uses, ask "Why are we doing it this way?" If the answer is "Because we've always done it this way," respond with "Well, how is it contributing to making us the best we can be?" If you don't get a satisfactory answer, eliminate or significantly improve the process or procedure so that it does contribute.

____ Hold a meeting with your constituents and ask them what really annoys them about the team's situation, environment, etc. Commit to changing three of the most frequently mentioned items that are hindering success.

_____ Go shopping for ideas. Visit a local business—anything from a restaurant to a machine shop. Don't come back until you see one thing that the business does very well and that your team could and should copy. Then follow through.

_____ Set up a pilot project for an innovative way of doing something for which the team is responsible. Try it on a small scale first. Learn from it. Try some more.

_____ Praise risk takers. Give them the opportunity to talk about their experiences and share the lessons they've learned.

_____ Stand up for your beliefs, even if you're a minority of one.

_____ What else can you do to challenge the status quo?

_____ What else can you do to experiment with new ways of doing things?

_____ What other ways can you find to support your constituents as they seek challenging opportunities and experiment with new ways of doing things?

Learning from Others

____ Identify a couple of successful people in your organization who excel at Challenging the Process. Interview them about what they think are the ingredients for innovation and experimentation. Ask them how they "get away with" challenging the status quo.

____ Identify a couple of successful people in other organizations who excel at Challenging the Process. Interview them, too.

____ Follow a challenger as he or she goes about daily activities. Make notes about what this person does.

____ Read biographies about a couple of revolutionaries in business, science, politics, religion, or any endeavor. Learn whatever you can from the accounts of their lives.

Learning in the Classroom or on Your Own

____ Read a book from the recommended list for Challenging the Process (see Appendix A).

____ Take a course in creative problem solving.

____ Take a course in new-product development.

____ Take a course in process reengineering.

____ Spend time in an Outward Bound or similar wilderness-adventure program.

____ Take a class in a subject that you know nothing about. Take notes not only on the content of the course, but also on how it feels to go through the process.

____ What other courses can you take to experience new things? Which would represent risks for you?

IMPROVING IN INSPIRING A SHARED VISION

Leaders passionately believe that they can make a difference. They *envision the future,* creating ideal and unique images of what the organization can become. Through their magnetism and quiet persuasion, leaders *enlist others* in their dreams. They breathe life into visions and get people to see the exciting possibilities of the future.

Following are some suggestions on how to improve in Inspiring a Shared Vision. Put a check mark next to each one that could work for you. Below each idea you choose, write a brief note about a specific action you could take to implement that idea in your particular situation. Feel free to add ideas of your own.

Learning by Doing

____ Become a futurist. Join the World Futures Society. Read *American Demographics* or other magazines about future trends. Use the Internet to find a "futures" conference that you can attend. Make a list of what reputable people are predicting will happen in the next ten years. Look for patterns in these trends; figure out how your organization or team will be affected.

____ Ask yourself "Am I in the job *to do something* or am I in it *for something to do?*" If your answer is "To do something"—which we assume it will be— then write down what you want to accomplish while you're in your current job and why. Make sure you can answer this question: Five years from now, if you were bragging to someone about what you had accomplished in your current job, what would you say?

____ Envision yourself ten years from now. Write an article about how you've made a difference in the last decade—how you've contributed to your job, your organization or team, your family, your community.

____ Interview some of your constituents and ask them about their hopes, dreams, goals, and aspirations for the future. How do these relate to your own? How can you incorporate their aspirations into yours?

_____ Close your eyes and visualize yourself five years in the future. What will you be doing? What will those you work with be doing? What will your family be doing? What differences will there be in the ways that people work and live? Get as clear a picture as possible.

_____ Turn what you imagine about the future into a five- to ten-minute "vision speech" for your organization or team. Keep the written speech in your daily planner. Review it daily, revising and refining as you feel moved to do so.

_____ Read your vision speech to someone who will give you constructive feedback. Ask the person these questions: "Is the speech imaginative or conservative? Is it unique or ordinary? Does it evoke visual images? Is it oriented toward the future or toward the present? Does it offer a view that can be shared by others?"

_____ Deliver your vision speech at every opportunity: at team meetings, at company meetings, at club meetings, at home. Publish it and disseminate it widely. Ask people for feedback. Ask them specifically if they could see themselves as part of this future.

_____ Set aside time every week (or as often as possible) to talk about the future with your constituents. Make your vision of the future part of a team meeting, a working lunch, a conversation by the coffee machine, etc.

_____ Whenever possible, volunteer to stand up in front of a group and speak, even if it's just to introduce someone or make an announcement.

_____ What else can you do to clarify the kind of future you'd like people to create together?

_____ What else can you do to forecast what the future will be like or to scan for future trends? Can you set up an ongoing process?

_____ What else can you do to learn more about your constituents' needs and dreams?

_____ How can you get more input from your constituents on a shared vision?

Learning from Others

_____ Read a biography of a person who's considered to be visionary.

_____ Visit your local library or go to a store that sells CDs, tapes, and videos. Check out or buy and then listen to several famous speeches by leaders who've inspired a shared vision. One example is Martin Luther King's "I Have a Dream" speech. Learn everything you can from the masters.

_____ Watch the C-SPAN channel on television or attend a lecture given by a good speaker. Pick up a few tips on how to express yourself with conviction and enthusiasm. Another good idea is to watch a speaker who's boring and doesn't connect with the audience. Then you can make notes on what *not* to do.

____ Interview a speech writer. Ask him or her to share methods for constructing an inspirational speech.

____ Go to a concert or an opera. Observe how the conductor uses his or her body and energy to bring forth the best in others.

Learning in the Classroom or on Your Own

____ Read a book from the recommended list for Inspiring a Shared Vision (see Appendix A).

____ Join Toastmasters.

____ Take a course in giving effective presentations.

____ Take a course in interpersonal-communication skills.

____ Take singing lessons.

____ Take acting lessons.

IMPROVING IN ENABLING OTHERS TO ACT

Leaders *foster collaboration* and build spirited teams. They actively involve others. Leaders understand that mutual respect is what sustains extraordinary efforts; they strive to create an atmosphere of trust and human dignity. They *strengthen others,* making each person feel capable and powerful.

Following are some suggestions on how to improve in Enabling Others to Act. Put a check mark next to each one that could work for you. Below each idea you choose, write a brief note about a specific action you could take to implement that idea in your particular situation. Feel free to add ideas of your own.

Learning by Doing

____ Treat *every* job as a project. Instead of looking at a job as a linear series of tasks, think of it as a project involving people from a variety of functions. Ask yourself which people should be involved. Call them together at the beginning.

____ For the next two weeks, commit to replacing the word "I" with "we." As a leader you can't do the job alone; extraordinary things are accomplished as a result of team efforts, not individual efforts. "We" is an inclusive word that signals a commitment to teamwork and sharing. Use it liberally.

____ Volunteer to be the chairperson of a professional, civic, or industry association. Working with volunteers will teach you collaborative skills and give you opportunities to use them.

____ Ask others to share in important tasks. For example, if an important presentation is coming up, ask a promising young constituent to prepare and deliver it. Be available to coach and support that person.

____ Ask peers for their opinions and viewpoints. Share problems with them.

____ Hang out at the coffee machine first thing in the morning. You'll encounter several of your constituents and peers. Engage in conversations about how things are going in their lives outside work or outside the team.

____ Keep your door open. Closed doors send a signal that you don't want to interact with others; they breed distrust and suspicion.

____ Admit your mistakes. Say "I don't know." Show that you're willing to change your mind when someone comes up with a better idea.

____ On a weekly basis, share information about how your team is doing in terms of meeting its goals. People want to know how things are going. This information makes them feel more powerful.

____ Ask for volunteers. When you give people a choice about being a part of what's happening, they're much more likely to be committed to a project.

____ Publicize your constituents' work. At each meeting with constituents, shine the spotlight on at least one person. At your next meeting, tell a story about someone who truly exemplified what teamwork is all about.

____ What else can you do to enhance people's sense of contribution and self-worth?

___ What else can you do to make people feel more in control of their own lives?

___ What else can you do to develop cooperative relationships with your constituents, your peers, or with colleagues in other teams or units?

___ What else can you do to make yourself more accessible and open to others?

Learning from Others

___ Observe a human resources person as he or she conducts a meeting. Try facilitating rather than managing meetings.

___ Hire a personal coach to help you improve in a specific leadership practice or a specific sport. Pay attention to this person's approaches and techniques and then try some of them.

___ Interview the coach of a professional or amateur athletic team in your area. Ask how you might apply the coach's methods with your constituents.

____ Choose someone in your organization who's known as an exceptional "people person." Accompany and observe this person for a few hours. Ask for tips on how you can do better.

____ Periodically trade places with your constituents and do their work. This is a terrific way to develop empathy and understanding, which contribute to trust.

Learning in the Classroom or on Your Own

____ Read a book from the recommended list for Enabling Others to Act (see Appendix A).

____ Take a course in team building.

____ Take a course in listening skills.

____ Take a course on how to run group meetings.

____ Take a course on consulting skills.

____ Get on the Internet and join a chat room.

____ Try out some groupware, such as Lotus Notes® or Novell® GroupWise.™

____ Study a social movement (e.g., civil rights or women's suffrage) and find out how proponents encouraged others to become involved.

IMPROVING IN MODELING THE WAY

Leaders establish values about how constituents, peers, colleagues, and customers ought to be treated. They create standards of excellence and then *set an example* for others to follow. Because complex change can overwhelm people and stifle action, leaders plan milestones to reach along the way so that others can *achieve small wins*. They unravel bureaucracy, put up signposts, and create opportunities for victory.

Following are some suggestions on how to improve in Modeling the Way. Put a check mark next to each one that could work for you. Below each idea you choose, write a brief note about a specific action you could take to implement that idea in your particular situation. Feel free to add ideas of your own.

Learning by Doing

_____ Clarify your personal credo—the values or principles that you believe should guide your team. Make sure that you communicate your credo orally and in writing to your constituents. Post it prominently for everyone to see.

_____ Ask your constituents to write their credos and share them at one of your team meetings. Ask people to come to consensus about the values they're prepared to live out in their work. If you have a set of organizational values, compare your team's to the organization's. If there's any incompatibility, resolve it.

_____ Keep track of how you spend your time. Check to see whether your actions are consistent with your team's values. If you find inconsistency, figure out what you need to do to align your actions with the values.

_____ Be expressive—even emotional—about your beliefs. If you're proud of your constituents for living up to high performance standards, let *them* know. Then go brag about them to others. Tell stories about the ones who are living out values in memorable ways.

____ Keep your daily planner at hand. Write down your promises as you make them. Make sure that you review them daily and fulfill them on schedule. Also be sure to let others know that you've done what you said you'd do.

____ Do something dramatic to demonstrate your commitment to a team value. For instance, if creativity is a value, take everyone to a local toy store, buy a few kids' games, and spend a couple of hours playing them. Then spend an hour discussing what people learned about creativity that could be applied to their own or the team's work.

____ Set goals that are achievable. Tell your constituents what the key milestones are so that they can easily see their progress.

____ Make decisions visible. Use a centrally located bulletin board to post reminders of the team's decisions. Keep the board updated with information on progress.

____ Set a personal example for others by behaving in ways that demonstrate and reinforce your stated values. For example, if collaboration is one of your values, make sure that you act as a team player.

____ What else can you do to clarify your own and your constituents' values?

____ What else can you do to communicate and build consensus around values?

___ In what other ways can you pay attention to and personally set an example of your team's values?

___ What else can you do to set clear goals, make plans, and establish milestones for the projects you lead?

Learning from Others

___ Watch the film *Gandhi* with some colleagues. Afterward, discuss how Gandhi set an example for his followers.

___ Choose some other famous leader that you consider to be a role model. Learn whatever you can from that person by reading a biography or watching a film about him or her.

___ Ask several trusted colleagues to choose the two or three most credible people in your organization. Interview these people. Spend time with them.

___ Pay attention to what your constituents say is important to them. Then look for actions that are examples of living out their values. Look for contradictions as well. Keep in mind that your constituents will also be paying attention to whether your words and deeds are consistent!

_____ Visit a retail store that's widely acknowledged for its extraordinary customer service. Watch and listen to what the store employees do and say. Shop there and see how you're treated. Interview a couple of the employees about how the store got such a stellar reputation.

_____ Spend some time with someone you personally look to as a role model. Ask that person for advice on how to make behavior consistent with values.

Learning in the Classroom or on Your Own

_____ Read a book from the recommended list for Modeling the Way (see Appendix A).

_____ Take a group or self-directed course in clarifying personal values.

_____ Take a course in time management, especially one in which you're asked to keep track of how you spend your time and then check your activities for consistency with your values.

_____ Take a story-telling class. Practice telling stories every time you get the opportunity.

_____ Take a course in goal setting and action planning.

_____ Purchase and use software for personal productivity. This software can assist you in automating some of your time-management processes.

IMPROVING IN ENCOURAGING THE HEART

Getting extraordinary things done in organizations is hard work. To keep hope and determination alive, leaders *recognize contributions* that individuals make in the climb to the top. And because the members of every winning team need to share in the rewards of their efforts, leaders *celebrate accomplishments.* They make people feel like heroes.

Following are some suggestions on how to improve in Encouraging the Heart. Put a check mark next to each one that could work for you. Below each idea you choose, write a brief note about a specific action you could take to implement that idea in your particular situation. Feel free to add ideas of your own.

Learning by Doing

____ Ask yourself which of your constituents best embodies the team's values and priorities. Think of ways to praise that person in the weeks to come.

____ Plan a festive celebration for each small milestone that your team reaches. Don't wait until the whole project is finished to celebrate.

____ Tell a public story about one of your constituents who went above and beyond the call of duty.

____ Give your constituents tools that they can use to recognize one another, such as index cards or notepads printed with the message "You Made My Day." Create a culture in which peers recognize peers.

____ Make creative use of rewards. Use your imagination and have some fun. Give a giant light bulb to the person who has the best idea of the month—or chocolate candy to the person who makes things run "sweetly." Tailor ideas to your own team.

____ Say "thank you" when you appreciate something that someone has done.

____ Write thank-you notes. We've never heard anyone complain about being thanked too much, but we've heard lots of complaints about being thanked too little!

____ Provide feedback about results, and the sooner the better. Feedback can range from a simple "well done" to a detailed debriefing session on how the latest project went and what your constituents learned.

____ Be personally involved. If you don't attend your team's celebrations and parties, you're sending the message that you're not interested.

____ Set aside one day each year as a special celebration day for your team.

____ Create a "Hall of Fame" for your team—an area that recognizes all of the members who've done extraordinary things.

____ What else can you do to recognize and reward individual contributions?

____ What else can you do to celebrate team accomplishments?

Learning from Others

_____ Go to a local athletic event. Watch the cheerleaders and the players as they celebrate small wins and big victories. Learn what you can from them about enthusiasm and passion.

_____ Ask for advice and coaching from someone you know who's much better at Encouraging the Heart than you are.

_____ Ask your constituents and others how they would like to be recognized for their accomplishments or successes.

_____ Attend an award ceremony for someone in your community or organization and make notes on what you like about it. Try some of the same methods the next time you hold an award ceremony.

_____ When you're at a wedding or holiday celebration, make notes on what you like about the celebration. Apply these ideas to your situation.

_____ Talk to people in your organization who have a reputation for helping others to develop. Ask them how they encourage others to excel.

_____ Sit on a bench in a local park and watch children play. Observe how they encourage one another.

Learning in the Classroom or on Your Own

____ Read a book from the recommended list for Encouraging the Heart (see Appendix A).

____ Take an improvisational-theater class.

____ Take a class on creativity.

____ Take a course in drawing, painting, or photography.

____ Learn to use a software program that creates graphics.

____ Take a course in advertising.

CHAPTER 8

Making Action Plans

On the next two pages are two action-planning forms. Complete one form for each leadership practice in which you want to improve. (Remember that you shouldn't work on more than two practices at one time.)

Before you start filling out these forms, we recommend that you make several copies in case you need more than one sheet for one practice. Also, several months from now, you may find that you want to make new action plans to improve in other practices.

The form asks you to make decisions about:

- Your improvement goal (the specific objective you want to accomplish)

- Action items (the specific steps you'll take to meet your improvement goal)

- Measures of success (the evidence that will indicate you've succeeded)

- Completion dates (the dates by which you will have completed the action items and achieved your goal)

- Support (someone to whom you can turn for coaching, advice, and encouragement)

ACTION-PLANNING FORM

Leadership Practice	Improvement Goal	Action Items	Measures of Success	Completion Dates	Support

ACTION-PLANNING FORM

Leadership Practice	Improvement Goal	Action Items	Measures of Success	Completion Dates	Support

CHAPTER 9

Discussing Your LPI-IC Feedback with Others

In completing the LPI-IC process, you asked others to give you the gift of feedback about your leadership practices. When people offer feedback, they like to know whether you value this gift, whether it was useful, and what you intend to do with it.

By sharing your LPI-IC feedback, you can tell people what they need to know and, at the same time, put all of the five practices to work for you:

Challenging the Process. Openly discussing your own leadership behavior may be something entirely new for you. But whether it's a new experience or not, it certainly gives you a chance to take a risk and make yourself vulnerable.

Inspiring a Shared Vision. When you share your feedback, you have a chance to talk about your hopes and dreams for the future as you improve your leadership abilities.

Enabling Others to Act. Sharing your feedback says "I trust you with this information about me. All of us belong to this team, and we're all trying to improve together. I can't do it alone."

Modeling the Way. Sharing your feedback sets the kind of example you'd like others to follow: being open about information that's relevant to improving the team. You are living the values of honesty, trust, and teamwork.

Encouraging the Heart. When you genuinely thank people for giving you feedback, you recognize their contributions. You can also thank them by providing coffee, juice, and muffins!

So we encourage you to share your feedback with those who gave you this gift. And we encourage you to use this sharing as a way to improve further in each of the leadership practices.

SHARING IN A GROUP OR
IN ONE-ON-ONE SESSIONS

Either you can invite all those who gave you feedback to a group meeting, or you can schedule a one-on-one meeting with each of them. In deciding which alternative to choose, consider your own comfort level, the norms of your organization (if applicable), and the comfort level of those who gave you the feedback.

Feedback meetings can be tough, but they can also benefit both you and your constituents. Just the fact that you're making the effort to share your LPI-IC feedback will mean a lot to people.

GUIDELINES FOR THE MEETING

Following these guidelines will increase your chances of having a meeting that's beneficial to everyone:

1. Prepare yourself. Develop an agenda so that you can keep the meeting focused and on track. Plan what you want to say and how you want to say it. Plan how you'll inform people and involve them. Refer to your action plan(s) so that you can include specific information about what you're going to do as a result of the feedback. If you need help, ask a consultant or human resources person to coach you ahead of time or attend the feedback meeting.

2. Schedule the meeting. It's best to share feedback in an organized fashion, so set up the group meeting or the individual sessions ahead of time.

3. Protect anonymity. The people who gave you feedback assumed that their individual scores would remain anonymous. The only exception is your manager. So under no circumstances should you ask people to disclose who gave you which scores. Nor should people be pressured by others to disclose, which means that you must intervene if this happens. If people volunteer their scores, that's another matter; then it's their choice.

4. Express your gratitude. Begin the discussion by saying "thank you." Let people know that you appreciate their feedback and their willingness to talk with you further about it. Make people feel comfortable.

5. Set ground rules. At the beginning of the meeting, establish a few ground rules. Let people know how the meeting will run, how long it will take, and what will be discussed. Also let them know what you expect from them, such as further information about specific things that you can do more of or less of (review your notes in Chapter 5 about additional information you needed). Finally, establish some rules about dealing with feedback during the meeting. (See "Ground Rules for Feedback" in this chapter.)

6. Describe the leadership model. Give a brief overview of the five practices. The descriptions in Chapters 2 and 7 can be used for this purpose.

7. Express your feelings. Let people know how you feel about the feedback you received. By expressing your feelings, you will more easily establish trust and rapport.

8. Show your scores. If you're sharing your actual scores (and we highly recommend that you do), either display them on overhead transparencies or distribute copies. If you choose not to show the scores, give an oral summary or distribute copies of a written summary.

9. Talk about strengths (highest scores). Start with what you do well, according to the observers. Cite specific examples: "My highest ratings were in the practice of Enabling Others to Act. I think I demonstrated this practice when I asked Leslie and Tom to take charge of planning the charity ball this year. That's an example of Enabling." Ask people to share their own specific examples of how you've demonstrated the practice. Then ask them how you can become even better.

10. Talk about opportunities for improvement (lowest scores). Define your understanding and perception of the feedback. Cite examples of instances in which you may not have done as well as you could. Ask others for specific examples. Then get feedback on how you can improve.

11. Discuss the practice that shows the largest gap between your LPI-IC: Self and LPI-IC: Observer scores. Ask people to help you understand why there's such a difference between your perceptions of yourself and their perceptions of you. For example, you might ask "What do I do that contributes to being misunderstood?" or "What am I missing? Is there something I do that accounts for this difference in perception?"

12. Ask for any other feedback and suggestions. Encourage people to contribute their ideas. You need their help if you and they are to be effective together.

13. Share your action plan(s). Tell people specifically what you plan to do over the next several weeks to improve. Ask them to hold you accountable and to give you positive reinforcement when they see that you're doing what you said you would do. (It's important that you get positive reinforcement along the way.) Let people know that you probably won't get new behaviors entirely right the first time, but that you'll keep trying and learning.

14. Encourage people to get feedback on their own leadership practices. Express your appreciation to them for their willingness to give you feedback and to participate in the discussion of your LPI-IC results. Then, if applicable, encourage them to do the same. Now that they've seen how helpful feedback can be, urge them to take advantage of the LPI-IC process. Explain that it doesn't matter whether they're managers or not: Everyone has to function as a leader at some point, and everyone can benefit from learning how to be a better leader.

Ground Rules for Feedback

In general, you'll need to pay special attention to the rules for receiving feedback, and your constituents will need to pay special attention to the rules for giving feedback. However, it's a good idea to discuss the rules for both giving and receiving feedback, because these activities represent essential team skills that you and your constituents need to develop in order to work together effectively.

In addition to explaining these rules, you should post a copy of them prominently. If you want, you may distribute individual copies as well.

Rules for Giving Feedback

1. Acknowledge aloud that it's tough to give honest feedback.

2. Avoid personal attacks.

3. Focus on specific behaviors—not attitudes, characterizations, or personalities. For example, say "When you cut me off in last week's meeting, I felt powerless" instead of "You're really rude."

4. Connect behaviors to results. For example, say "When you don't follow through on your commitment to be at meetings on time, I get behind in my own work and have to work overtime to catch up. That makes me less efficient in my work."

5. Avoid hearsay, accusations, and exaggerations. Relate only what you have personally experienced. Let others speak for themselves.

6. Provide information that's constructive: "If you had acknowledged that you received those improvement ideas I left in your in-basket, I would have felt that I was being listened to."

7. Include positive as well as negative feedback. People need to know what they're doing well in order to believe that they can improve. They also need to know what success looks like in order to have goals.

Rules for Receiving Feedback

1. Acknowledge aloud that it's tough to receive feedback.

2. Approach feedback as a *partnership process*, not a debate.

3. Focus energy on understanding the behavior being discussed, not fixing it right then and there. You might need time to consider alternatives, gather more information, check facts, and so on.

4. Don't be reluctant to ask questions to gain a better understanding of the feedback. Request specific examples so that you'll know which behaviors people are referring to.

5. Confirm your understanding: "If I understand correctly, you're saying. . . ."

6. Take feedback seriously. Bring a notepad and take notes.

7. Seek a balance between positive and negative feedback. If you receive only positive feedback, ask about practices or behaviors in which you could improve. If you receive only negative feedback, ask about practices or behaviors in which you're strong.

APPENDIX A

Recommended Readings

CHALLENGING THE PROCESS

Calvert, G. (1993). *Highwire management: Risk-taking tactics for leaders, innovators, and trailblazers.* San Francisco: Jossey-Bass.

Csikszentmihalyi, M. (1990). *Flow: The psychology of optimal experience.* New York: HarperCollins.

Jaffe, D.T., Scott, C.D., & Tobe, G.R. (1994). *Rekindling commitment: How to revitalize yourself, your work, and your organization.* San Francisco: Jossey-Bass.

Kanter, R.M. (1983). *The change masters: Innovation for productivity in the American corporation.* New York: Simon & Schuster.

Kriegel, R., & Patler, L. (1991). *If it ain't broke...break it!* New York: Warner.

Peters, T. (1992). *Liberation management: Necessary disorganization for the nanosecond nineties.* New York: Knopf.

INSPIRING A SHARED VISION

Bennis, W., & Nanus, B. (1985). *Leaders: The strategies for taking charge.* New York: HarperCollins.

Hamel, G., & Prahalad, C.K. (1994). *Competing for the future: Breakthrough strategies for seizing control of your industry and creating the markets of tomorrow.* Boston: Harvard Business School Press.

Nanus, B. (1992). *Visionary leadership: Creating a compelling sense of direction for your organization.* San Francisco: Jossey-Bass.

Pearce, T. (1995). *Leading out loud.* San Francisco: Jossey-Bass.

Peck, M.S. (1978). *The road less traveled.* New York: Simon & Schuster.

Quigley, J.V. (1993). *Vision: How leaders develop it, share it and sustain it.* New York: McGraw-Hill.

Schwartz, F. (1991). *The art of the long view.* New York: Currency.

Wheatley, M. (1992). *Leadership and the new science.* San Francisco: Berrett-Koehler.

ENABLING OTHERS TO ACT

Block, P. (1987). *The empowered manager: Positive political skills at work.* San Francisco: Jossey-Bass.

Case, J. (1995). *Open-book management: The coming business revolution.* New York: HarperCollins.

Fisher, R., & Ury, W. (1981). *Getting to yes.* Boston: Houghton Mifflin.

Hakim, C. (1994). *We are all self-employed.* San Francisco: Berrett-Koehler.

Helgesen, S. (1995). *The web of inclusion.* New York: Currency.

Lawler, E.E., III. (1992). *The ultimate advantage: Creating the high-involvement organization.* San Francisco: Jossey-Bass.

Pfeffer, J. (1994). *Competitive advantage through people: Unleashing the power of the work force.* Boston: Harvard Business School Press.

Stack, J. (1992). *The great game of business: The only sensible way to run a company.* New York: Currency.

Tannen, D. (1994). *Talking from 9 to 5: How women's and men's conversational styles affect who gets heard, who gets credit, and what gets done at work.* New York: William Morrow.

Wellins, R.E., Byham, W.C., & Wilson, J.M. (1991). *Empowered teams: Creating self-directed work groups that improve quality, productivity, and participation.* San Francisco: Jossey-Bass.

MODELING THE WAY

Armstrong, D. (1992). *Managing by storying around: A new method of leadership.* New York: Currency.

Collins, J., & Porras, J. (1994). *Built to last: Successful habits of visionary companies.* New York: HarperCollins.

DePree, M. (1989). *Leadership is an art.* New York: Doubleday.

DePree, M. (1992). *Leadership jazz.* New York: Doubleday.

Kouzes, J.M., & Posner, B.Z. (1993). *Credibility: How leaders gain and lose it, why people demand it.* San Francisco: Jossey-Bass.

Schwarzkopf, H.N., with Pietre, P. (1992). *It doesn't take a hero.* New York: Bantam.

ENCOURAGING THE HEART

Deal, T.E., & Jenkins, W.A. (1994). *Managing the hidden organization: Strategies for empowering your behind-the-scenes employees.* New York: Warner.

Kohn, A. (1993). *Punished by rewards.* New York: Houghton Mifflin.

Nelson, B. (1994). *1001 ways to reward employees.* New York: Workman.

Peterson, C., & Bossio, L.M. (1991). *Health and optimism: New research on the relationship between positive thinking and physical well-being.* New York: Free Press.

Seligman, M. (1990). *Learned optimism.* New York: Knopf.

Vroom, V.H. (1994). *Work and motivation.* San Francisco: Jossey-Bass.

OTHER BOOKS ON LEADERSHIP

Bennis, W. (1989). *On becoming a leader.* Reading, MA: Addison-Wesley.

Bass, B.M., & Stodgill, R.M. (1990). *Bass & Stodgill's handbook of leadership.* New York: Free Press.

Gardner, H. (1995). *Leading minds.* New York: HarperCollins.

Gardner, J. (1989). *On leadership.* New York: Free Press.

Heifetz, R.A. (1994). *Leadership without easy answers.* Cambridge, MA: Belknap.

Peters, T., & Austin, N. (1983). *A passion for excellence: The leadership difference.* New York: Random House.

APPENDIX B

Instructions for Hand Scoring[7]

On the following pages are five grids (one for each practice) that you can use to record your LPI-IC scores. The first grid, which is for Challenging the Process, asks you to record scores for LPI-IC items 1, 6, 11, 16, 21, and 26. These are the items that relate to behaviors involved in Challenging the Process. An abbreviated form of each item is printed beside the grid as a handy reference. Each of the remaining four grids is constructed in the same way, listing abbreviations of the LPI-IC items that pertain to that practice.

To record your LPI-IC: Self and LPI-IC: Observer scores for each practice, transfer the numbers from the response sheets to the scoring grid. Under the heading "Self Rating," record the scores that you gave yourself.

Under the heading "Observers' Ratings" you'll notice that there are enough columns to accommodate twenty observers. Record each observer's ratings in one of the columns.

If you have separate observer categories, fill in the blanks for *observer column headings* with "M" for your manager's scores, "C1" for the first constituent whose scores you record, "C2" for the second constituent, "P1" for the first peer, "P2" for the second peer, "O1" for the first other observer, "O2" for the second other observer, and so on. If you don't have observer categories, fill in the column headings with "O1," "O2," and so on for other observers.

After you've recorded all scores for Challenging the Process, total each column and write the sums in the row marked "Totals." Transfer your self total to the blank marked "Self Total." Then add all of the observers' totals. (Don't include the self total.) Write this grand total in the blank marked "Total of All Observers' Scores." To obtain the average observer score, divide the grand total by the number of observers. Then write this average in the blank marked "Observer Average." Figure 8 shows how the grid would look if scores for self and five observers had been entered.

After you've filled in the grids, it's a good idea to make copies of them so that you can place the copies next to the pages in Chapter 5 and refer to your scores easily as you analyze your feedback.

---

[7]*If your LPI-IC: Self and LPI-IC: Observer forms are being computer scored, ignore this appendix.*

CHALLENGING THE PROCESS

	SELF RATING	OBSERVERS' RATINGS																		Total of All Observers' Scores
		M	D₁	D₂	C₁	C₂														
1. Seeks challenging opportunities	5	4	2	5	4	1														
6. Challenges people to try new approaches	4	4	3	4	4	2														
11. Looks outside organization for ways to improve	3	3	5	1	1	1														
16. Asks "What can we learn?"	4	2	1	1	5	3														
21. Experiments and takes risks	2	5	2	3	2	5														
26. Takes initiative to overcome obstacles	5	1	3	2	3	2														
TOTALS	23	19	16	16	19	14														84

Self Total: _____23_____

Observer Average: _____16.8_____

FIGURE 8. Sample Completed Grid

CHALLENGING THE PROCESS

	SELF RATING	OBSERVERS' RATINGS																			Total of All Observers' Scores
1. Seeks challenging opportunities																					
6. Challenges people to try new approaches																					
11. Looks outside organization for ways to improve																					
16. Asks "What can we learn?"																					
21. Experiments and takes risks																					
26. Takes initiative to overcome obstacles																					
TOTALS																					

Self Total: _____

Observer Average: _____

INSPIRING A SHARED VISION

	SELF RATING	OBSERVERS' RATINGS																Total of All Observers' Scores
2. Talks about future trends																		
7. Describes compelling image of future																		
12. Appeals to others to share dream of future																		
17. Shows others how their interests can be realized																		
22. Is enthusiastic and positive about future																		
27. Speaks with conviction about meaning of work																		
TOTALS																		

Self Total: _____

Observer Average: _____

ENABLING OTHERS TO ACT

	SELF RATING	OBSERVERS' RATINGS																							Total of All Observers' Scores
3. Develops cooperative relationships																									
8. Listens to diverse points of view																									
13. Treats people with dignity and respect																									
18. Supports other people's decisions																									
23. Lets people choose how to do their work																									
28. Ensures that people grow in their jobs																									
TOTALS																									

Self Total: _____

Observer Average: _____

MODELING THE WAY

	SELF RATING	OBSERVERS' RATINGS																						Total of All Observers' Scores
4. Sets example of what is expected																								
9. Ensures that people adhere to agreed-on standards																								
14. Follows through on promises and commitments																								
19. Is clear about his/her philosophy of leadership																								
24. Ensures that goals, plans, milestones are set																								
29. Makes progress toward goals one step at a time																								
TOTALS																								

Self Total: _____   Observer Average: _____

ENCOURAGING THE HEART

	SELF RATING	OBSERVERS' RATINGS																					Total of All Observers' Scores
5. Praises people for a job well done																							
10. Expresses confidence in people's abilities																							
15. Creatively rewards people for their contributions																							
20. Recognizes people for commitment to shared values																							
25. Finds ways to celebrate accomplishments																							
30. Gives team members appreciation and support																							
TOTALS																							

Self Total: _____

Observer Average: _____

PERCENTILE RANKINGS FOR LPI-IC RATINGS

The chart on the opposite page represents the percentile rankings for 6,000 people in Kouzes and Posner's database of more than 12,000 leaders and 70,000 observers since 1986. This ranking is determined by the percentage of people who score at or below a given number. For example, if your score for "challenging" is at the 70th percentile line on the chart, this means that you scored higher than 70 percent of all the people who have taken the LPI-IC. You would be in the top 30 percent on that dimension.

Put an "S" through the number in each column that corresponds to the number of your LPI-IC Self Total score on that practice. Connect these five "S"s with a heavy line. Put an "O" through the number in each column that corresponds to the "LPI-IC Observer Average" for each practice. (While you may have separate observer categories, we recommend, for visual clarity, plotting only the Observer Average, obtained by dividing the total of all observers' scores by the number of observers.) Connect the 5 "O"s with a dotted line. This will give you a graphic representation of your LPI percentile ranking, illustrating the relationship between your self perception and the observations of other people.

Our studies indicate that a "high" score is one at the 70th percentile or above. A "low" score is one at the 30th percentile or below. A score that falls between those ranges would be considered a "moderate" score.

As you look at the graph of your LPI-IC scores—and those from the LPI-IC Observers—consider where they agree and disagree. Do the lines follow each other in a parallel fashion?

LPI-IC PERCENTILE RANKINGS

Percentile	Challenging	Inspiring	Enabling	Modeling	Encouraging
100	60	60	60	60	60
	58 59	57 58 59	59	58 59	59
	57	56	58	57	
	56	55		56	58
			57		57
	55	54		55	
	54	53	56		56
		52		54	
90	53		55		55
	52	51		53	54
		50	54		
	51				53
80	50			52	
		49	53		52
	49			51	51
		48			
70			52		50
	48			50	
		47			49
	47	46	51	49	
60	46	45			48
		44	50		
	45	43		48	47
50	44	42	49	47	46
					45
	43	41	48	46	44
40	42	40	47	45	43
	41	39			
30		38		44	42
	40	37	46	43	41
	39	36			40
20	38	35	45	42	39
	37	34 33	44	41	38
	36	32	43	40	37
	35	31	42	39	36 35
10	34	30 29	41 40	38	34 33
	33	28 27	39 38	37 36	32 31
	32 31	26 25	37 36	35	29 30
	30 29	24	35	33 34	28
	28	20 21 22 23		31 32	25 26 27
1	24 25 26 27	16 17 18 19	32 33 34	29 30	21 22 23 24

FOR HELP

If you find that you need additional help with the LPI-IC or your LPI-IC feedback, contact:

> Customer Service
> Jossey-Bass/Pfeiffer
> 350 Sansome Street
> San Francisco, CA 94104–1342
> Telephone: (415) 433–1740 or (800) 274–4434
> Fax: (415) 433–0499 or (800) 569–0433